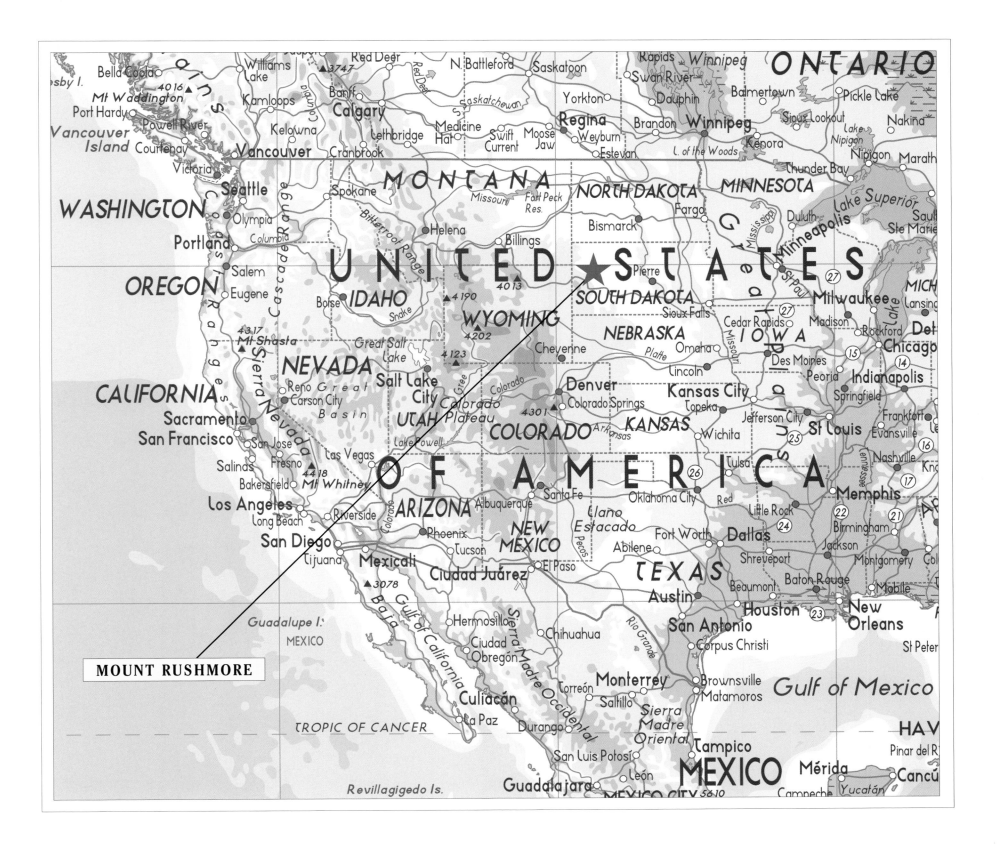

MOUNT RUSHMORE

Published by Creative Education
123 South Broad Street
Mankato, Minnesota 56001

Creative Education is an imprint of The Creative Company.

Designed by Stephanie Blumenthal
Production design by Melinda Belter
Art direction by Rita Marshall

Photographs by Alamy (ACE STOCK LIMITED, Robert E. Barber, Carphotos, Danita Delimont, Elmtree Images, EuroStyle Graphics, Folio Inc, franzfoto.com, Robert Fried, GC Minerals, Bill Howe, Images Etc Ltd, Andre Jenny, Ana Licuanan, Manor Photography, nagelstock.com, Peter Arnold, Inc., Photo Network, les polders, POPPERFOTO, GEORGE AND MONSERRATE SCHWARTZ, Stock Connection Distribution, Tom Till, Visions of America, LLC, Andrew Woodley), Corbis (Phil Schermeister), Design Maps, Inc., Getty Images (Kevin Eilbeck, Frederic Lewis, Bobby Model, F.A. Rinehart / Hulton Archive, Time Life Pictures National Park Service / Mount Rushmore National Memorial / Time Life Pictures)

Printed in the United States of America

Library of Congress Cataloging-in-Publication Data
Bodden, Valerie.
Mount Rushmore / by Valerie Bodden.
p. cm. — (Modern wonders of the world)
Includes index.
ISBN-13: 978-1-58341-440-8
1. Mount Rushmore National Memorial (S.D.)—Juvenile literature. 2. Mount Rushmore National Memorial (S.D.)—History—Juvenile literature. 3. Borglum, Gutzon, 1867-1941—Juvenile literature. I. Title. II. Series.

F657.R8B63 2006   978.3'93—dc22   2005051779

First edition

2 4 6 8 9 7 5 3 1

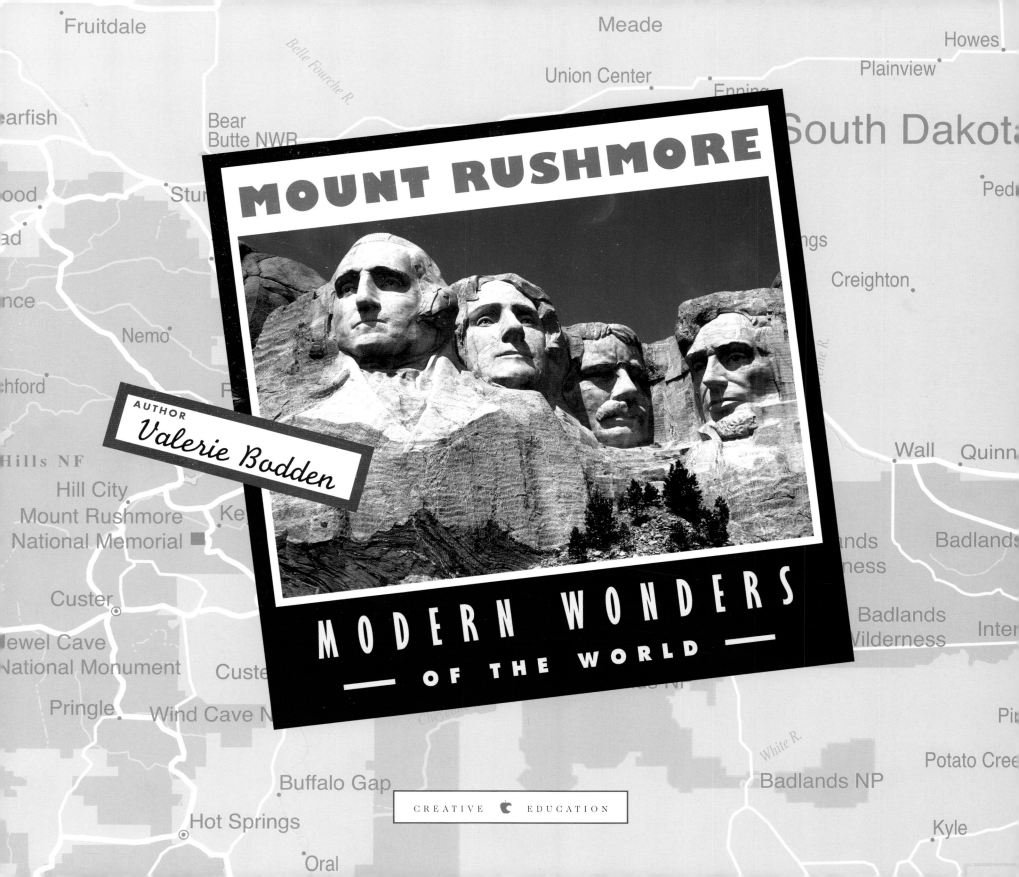

MOUNT RUSHMORE

AUTHOR
Valerie Bodden

MODERN WONDERS
OF THE WORLD

CREATIVE EDUCATION

MOUNT  RUSHMORE

For more than half a century, the immense head of George Washington (opposite) has kept watch over the mountains and grasslands of South Dakota, where bison and other animals roam freely.

His head is 80 times larger than that of the average human. Each eye is 11 feet (3.4 m) across. His nose is longer than the entire face of Egypt's Great Sphinx. If he were full-length, he would tower 465 feet (142 m) above the ground, dwarfing the Statue of Liberty. One-fourth of one of the largest sculptures in the world, the colossal head of George Washington stares out from the strong granite of Mount Rushmore. Next to him peer the faces of Thomas Jefferson, Abraham Lincoln, and Theodore Roosevelt. The four heads, carved into the Black Hills of South Dakota, have been admired for generations, not only as works of art, but as timeless symbols of America.

THE SHRINE OF DEMOCRACY

The most dramatic way to approach Mount Rushmore is from the southeast via the Iron Mountain Road, which passes through several narrow granite tunnels that serve as natural picture frames for the monument. The nearby Needles Highway provides spectacular views of an area of granite spires known as the "Needles."

The Mount Rushmore National Memorial has its origins in the early 1920s, a time of great optimism and growth in America. The country had just emerged from World War I as a rich and powerful nation. New inventions, from radios to refrigerators, made everyday life easier and more efficient. Roads were being improved, and—as people found themselves with extra spending money —tourism was on the rise.

In 1923, eager to have his state cash in on the booming tourism industry, Doane Robinson, secretary and historian of the South Dakota Historical Society, came

up with the idea to carve a huge sculpture in South Dakota's scenic Black Hills region. He enlisted the help of fellow South Dakotan Peter Norbeck, a United States senator, and together they created a plan to seek funds for the project from the federal government and private citizens.

A year later, Robinson asked 57-year-old American sculptor Gutzon Borglum to design the sculpture and supervise the project. Borglum, who had studied art in Paris under famous French sculptor Auguste Rodin, jumped at the opportunity. For years, Borglum had been urging artists to create art on a large scale, and this was just the type of project he loved.

6

In the early 1920s, many Americans were purchasing their first cars; Ford Model-Ts (opposite far left) were especially popular. With their new-found mobility, people took to the roads, and some traveled to the Needles (left) area of the Black Hills. Today, granite tunnels (opposite center) add a unique element to the region's roadways.

Mount Rushmore was named for Charles E. Rushmore, a New York City lawyer who traveled to the Black Hills in the 1880s. When Rushmore asked the name of the mountain, locals jokingly said they would call it Rushmore. The name stuck, and Rushmore later donated $5,000 to the Mount Rushmore monument.

In 1925, Borglum scouted the Black Hills, searching for the right mountain on which to carve his masterpiece. He inspected one peak after another, rejecting them all until he came to Mount Rushmore. Rising to an altitude of 5,725 feet (1,745 m), with a granite face 1,000 feet (305 m) long and 400 feet (122 m) high, Mount Rushmore was the highest peak in the immediate vicinity and provided ample room for the sculpture Borglum had in mind.

In addition, the mountain faced southeast, meaning that the sun would light the sculpture for most of the day.

Although Robinson had originally envisioned a sculpture honoring famous Western figures—explorers such as Meriwether Lewis and William Clark or Indian chiefs such as Red Cloud—Borglum rejected that idea. In order to attract tourists from around the nation, he felt that the sculpture should reflect national, rather than local, heroes. At the same time, the fiercely patriotic sculptor wanted to erect a monument that would tell the story of America.

Although Borglum chose four U.S. presidents—George Washington, Thomas Jefferson, Abraham Lincoln, and Theodore Roosevelt—as the subjects of his sculpture, his desire was not to erect a memorial specifically to those men, but rather to the social and political **ideals** they represented.

Rather than honoring local heroes such as Sioux Indian chief Red Cloud (opposite far left), Gutzon Borglum wished to create a sculpture of national importance, much like the Statue of Liberty (opposite center). Borglum was dedicated to the principles on which America was founded, so powerfully expressed in the country's Declaration of Independence (left).

Gutzon Borglum's sculpting of Thomas Jefferson (opposite) reflected his admiration for the man who had helped to open the West to exploration with the purchase of the Louisiana Territory. Some of the lands in the territory, including South Dakota, were found to be rich in gold deposits.

Washington (president 1789–97), in his role as first president and a key figure in the creation of the Constitution, represented the spirit of government by the people. Jefferson (1801–09), who had written the Declaration of Independence and doubled the size of the U.S. through the **Louisiana Purchase**, stood for belief in the dignity of the common man, as well as the nation's growth and prosperity. Lincoln (1861–65) represented unity for his efforts to preserve the union during the Civil War and his role in bringing an end to the practice of slavery. Roosevelt (1901–09)—whose inclusion on the monument stirred controversy, as some people felt he wasn't as important as the other three figures—represented the connecting of **East** and **West** for his part in the creation of the **Panama Canal**.

With both his site and his subjects selected, Borglum was ready to begin work on his monument to America. In 1925, the U.S. Congress designated Mount Rushmore a national memorial. Two years later, as the first drilling finally took place on the mountain, President Calvin Coolidge referred to the monument as a "shrine." The name would stick, as the memorial would soon be nicknamed "The Shrine of Democracy."

Gutzon Borglum modeled Thomas Jefferson's face as it looked at the age of 33, before he became president. Most people were unfamiliar with how Jefferson had looked at that age, and many mistook his face for Martha Washington, George's wife, while it was being carved!

The granite of the Black Hills is rich with minerals such as aquamarine (right). As workers shaped the rock of Mount Rushmore into the enormous presidential heads, they often came across mineral deposits, which they had to carefully work around.

The Black Hills—which are actually low, rounded mountains—rise at the edge of the Great Plains of South Dakota. Their slopes are covered with ponderosa pines, whose dark needles make the mountains look black from a distance. Deer, elk, and antelope roam this 6,000-square-mile (15,500 sq km) mountain range, and precious minerals such as copper, silver, **aquamarine**, and gold can be found within its stones. At the core of the mountains is granite, a hard **igneous** rock.

Shaping the granite of Mount Rushmore into the heads of four American icons was a painstaking task. First, Borglum created a five-foot-tall (1.5 m) scale model of the heads, with one inch (2.5 cm) on the model equaling one foot (30.5 cm) on the mountain. Then, in October 1927, Borglum began work on George Washington.

Dynamite was used to create a 60-foot-high (18 m) oval shape for Washington's head. Once the basic shape had been formed, workers constructed a tool made of a large **protractor**, ruler, and **plumb line**. They then used this tool to transfer precise measurements from the model to the sculpture, painting numbers on the rock to show how much stone needed to be removed. After the measurements were marked, drillers

Mount Rushmore's progress is well-documented in photographs, thanks to the Eastman Kodak Company. As part of its experiments with different kinds of film in the 1930s, the company provided Gutzon Borglum's son Lincoln with elaborate cameras and color film to test on the scenery and lighting conditions of the Black Hills.

Workers on Mount Rushmore were constantly exposed to hard, grainy granite dust. At times, their faces and clothes were so covered with dust that it looked like they had been working in a snowstorm. Although masks were provided, workers rarely used them, and some later died of the lung disease silicosis.

made holes for dynamite charges, which were used to take off the excess rock.

Once dynamite had removed the rock to within about six inches (15 cm) of the final carving surface, workers drilled holes very close together in the granite. This weakened the rock enough that the pieces could be removed with hammers. Finally, the drill holes were smoothed away to create an even, white surface. The same process was followed for each of the heads, Jefferson beginning in 1930, Lincoln in 1931, and Roosevelt in 1936. As work on the monument pro-

gressed, Borglum had to constantly rearrange his plans for the sculpture in order to avoid flaws and imperfections in the stone. Originally, Borglum had wanted to place Jefferson to Washington's right. After work on Jefferson's head had begun, however, workers discovered that there was insufficient stone in that location. So Borglum had the Jefferson head blasted off and begun again to Washington's left.

At one time or another, more than 350 men worked on the mountain. Usually 30 to 70 men worked at a time, measuring, drilling, and blasting the rock, and sharpening drill bits. The men, mostly local unemployed loggers, ranchers, and miners,

Many of the men who worked on Mount Rushmore had been hard-rock miners and were skilled in the use of dynamite. Their expertise enabled Gutzon Borglum to create remarkably lifelike representations of all four presidents, including Roosevelt (left), who was sculpted as he looked in 1918, a year before his death.

Visitors to Mount Rushmore are likely to see an abundance of wildlife. From chipmunks and squirrels to mountain goats and bighorn sheep, a number of animals make their homes near the monument. Turkey vultures and bald eagles fly overhead, and wildflowers such as black-eyed Susans and snapdragons decorate the mountainside.

stayed in a bunkhouse at the bottom of the mountain. Until 1936, when a cable car was added to carry workers to the top of the mountain, they began the workday with a half-hour climb up a 760-step stairway.

During the beginning stages of work on each head, the men hung from the top of the mountain in harnesses made of steel and leather. They were raised and lowered by hand-operated **winches**. As work progressed, they stood on scaffolding attached to the figures. Amazingly, despite working high above the ground using heavy equipment and dynamite, no workers were killed or permanently injured in the course of the project.

Shortly after work on Mount Rushmore began, the **Great Depression** struck America. As a result, it was often difficult to raise funds for the project. Whenever money ran out—which happened quite frequently—work on the sculpture had to be shut down, sometimes for up to a year at a time. Finally, in October 1941—seven months after Borglum's death—the enormous sculpture was completed. Ultimately, the project cost almost $1 million. The federal government provided $836,000 of the total, and private donors supplied the rest of the funds. Borglum himself was the largest private contributor, giving $7,000 to the project.

Although a tourist attraction, Mount Rushmore is also a haven for wildlife, including bald eagles (opposite far left) and bighorn sheep (top), as well as plants, such as yellow coneflowers (bottom right). Farther east, on the edge of the Black Hills, prairie dogs (opposite center) and yucca (bottom left) thrive on South Dakota's prairies.

AN ENDURING WONDER

Today, National Park Service inspectors hang from the side of Mount Rushmore in harnesses (opposite) much like those used by the monument's original creators. Only a few miles away, Harney Peak (right), the highest point in the U.S. east of the Rocky Mountains, offers visitors a spectacular view of the surrounding Black Hills.

During the years of work on Mount Rushmore, Gutzon Borglum staged several dedication ceremonies in order to attract attention to the project. Celebrations were held in 1925 when the site was dedicated, and again in 1927 when work on the mountain formally began. Each head was also dedicated as it neared completion—Washington in 1930, Jefferson in 1936, Lincoln in 1937, and Roosevelt in 1939. During the elaborate dedication ceremonies, which were attended by up to 12,000 spectators and often included bands, fireworks, and celebrities, the featured head was draped with a massive American flag that was removed with a dramatic flourish.

Although work on the monument was completed in 1941, the final dedication of the site didn't take place until 50 years later. On July 3, 1991, 19 of the men who had worked on the sculpture were present as President George H. W. Bush formally dedicated the memorial, noting that when its builders "dusted themselves off after the last day's work, they had produced a living monument."

Today, National Park Service staff members annually inspect the Rushmore monument and seal any cracks. The Park Service has also installed a sophisticated monitoring system to detect any movement of the monument's rock. Although slight shifting of the stone due to temperature changes has been

Rather than a regular salary, Gutzon Borglum was paid 25 percent of all monies spent on the project, not to exceed $87,500. While this meant that when funds were low Borglum didn't get paid, in 1938, the sculptor earned $16,013, a huge amount during the Great Depression. By comparison, U.S. congressmen earned $10,000.

Although granite is a durable rock that weathers very slowly, extreme temperature conditions such as those found in the Black Hills can cause it to break apart. When water freezes in minute cracks in the rock, it expands, creating tremendous pressure and causing further cracking.

detected over the years, the sculpture is in no immediate danger.

Over the years, the National Park Service has improved the grounds of the memorial, which is now part of the Black Hills National Forest. In 1997, Mount Rushmore National Memorial Park was remodeled with an amphitheater, a museum, and a trail leading to the base of the sculpture.

In 1998, the National Park Service added another component to the park. Part of Borglum's original plan for the monument had been the creation of a Hall of Records, which would be carved into the canyon behind the faces and would hold copies of important

American documents. Due to a lack of funds, however, only the entranceway to the hall was carved in the 1930s. In 1998, the Park Service placed a vault containing the words of the U.S. Constitution and the Declaration of Independence, as well as information about Mount Rushmore, in the floor of the entranceway.

Many people who have not personally visited the Rushmore memorial have seen the monument on the big screen. Mount Rushmore has been featured in numerous movies, most famously Alfred Hitchcock's 1959 classic *North by Northwest*. The film stirred up controversy with its climactic chase scene across the

Since the September 11, 2001, terrorist attacks in New York and Washington, D.C., security at Mount Rushmore has been tightened. The rangers who patrol the park, along with those at other national parks, receive special training in the use of M-16 rifles and are trained in antiterrorism measures.

In 1948, American sculptor Korczak Ziolkowski began sculpting a monument of the famous Sioux chief Crazy Horse. Today, work on the Crazy Horse Memorial, located fewer than 20 miles (32 km) from Mount Rushmore, continues.

Although Sioux tepees no longer dot South Dakota's prairies, the Crazy Horse Memorial (bottom)—which, when completed, will be 10 times larger than Mount Rushmore—is a tribute to the Sioux.

sculpture. Although the scene was actually shot on a studio model of the monument, most viewers couldn't tell the difference, and many complained that it was a desecration of the memorial.

While many people revere Mount Rushmore, some Sioux Indians see it as a reminder of what they've lost. The land the monument stands on once belonged to the Sioux, but as America expanded westward during the 19th century, it was taken from them. Today, the Sioux continue to fight for the return of a portion of the Black Hills, sometimes protesting near the monument.

Despite such occasional controversy, Mount Rushmore has attracted tourists from the beginning. In 1930, about 400 people a day arrived to watch Borglum work. Today, the immense monument continues to attract visitors, with more than two million people a year journeying to the Black Hills to visit it. What they see is a masterpiece of engineering prowess and artistic achievement, as well as a breathtaking symbol of U.S. ideals. The monument's colossal faces look down on them from the solid granite of the Black Hills, enduring, as Borglum dreamed, "until wind and rain alone shall wear them away."

SEEING THE WONDER

Locations throughout Mount Rushmore National Memorial Park provide awe-inspiring views of the monument. Visitors can focus in on the sculpture's details with a glimpse through coin-operated binoculars. Or, they can peer up at the vast monument as they stroll along the Park's colorful Avenue of Flags (opposite).

Whether one arrives from across South Dakota or across the world, Mount Rushmore is an awe-inspiring attraction that draws millions of visitors. Tourists flying into South Dakota often land in Rapid City, which is located 25 miles (40 km) northeast of the monument. From there, rental cars or private tour companies can bring visitors to the memorial. There is no public transportation to the site.

There is no fee to view the monument, but visitors who drive to Mount Rushmore must pay an annual parking fee that cost $8 in 2006.

Although there is no camping at Mount Rushmore, there are several campgrounds in the Black Hills National Forest and nearby Custer State Park. Hotels are available in the towns of Keystone and Hill City, both within 10 miles (16 km) of the park, as well as in Rapid City.

Mount Rushmore National Memorial Park is open 24 hours a day year-round, although some buildings are open only during the daytime or in the summer. The park's Grand View Terrace viewing platform provides a stunning, unobstructed view of the monument. Leading up to the terrace is the impressive Avenue of Flags, lined

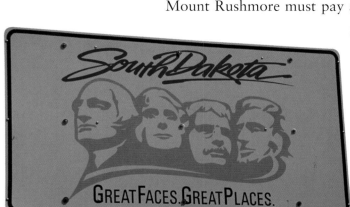

Over the course of the monument's creation, more than 450,000 tons (408,000 t) of rock were removed from Mount Rushmore. With America's entry into World War II in 1941, all plans to remove the rock fragments beneath the sculpture were abandoned. Today, a 300-foot-deep (90 m) pile of rock remains there.

South Dakota is a state of varied landscapes. Besides the Black Hills, the state is also home to the Badlands, an area of odd-shaped, soft rock formations. Much of South Dakota is covered with grasslands, and two of the longest **limestone** caves in the world are also found there.

From grasslands under a fiery sunset to Mount Rushmore under dazzling fireworks, South Dakota is a land of breathtaking and varied beauty.

with the flags of the 50 U.S. states and 6 U.S. **territories**. The Lincoln Borglum Museum, located below the terrace, features interactive exhibits and historical film footage of the monument being carved.

A short walk down the Presidential Trail, a half-mile (0.8 km) walking trail, provides the closest views of the monument, taking tourists near enough to touch the granite at the base of Mount Rushmore. The trail also leads to the Sculptor's Studio, which is open in the summer and features the original models and tools used in creating the monument. From May to September, visitors can witness the

evening lighting ceremony at 9:00 P.M. (8:00 P.M. in September) from the park's amphitheater. Although there is no lighting ceremony in the winter, the monument is lit every night.

Summer weather in the Black Hills is usually mild, with warm days and cool nights, although July and August are often hot. Winter temperatures tend to be higher than those in the rest of the state, although they sometimes drop below 0 °F (−18 °C). Snow can fall anytime from early September to mid-May. Layered clothing and comfortable walking shoes are recommended any time of year.

MOUNT  RUSHMORE

QUICK FACTS

Location: Southwestern South Dakota, 25 miles (40 km) southwest of Rapid City

Time of construction: October 1927 to October 1941

Dedication: Dedicated on October 1, 1925; the finished monument was formally dedicated on July 3, 1991, with a speech by President George H. W. Bush

Composition: Granite

Sculptor: Gutzon Borglum

Work force involved: More than 350 laborers

Dimensions of sculpture:

Height: 60 feet (18 m)

Width: 365 feet (111 m)

Dimensions of facial features:

Eyes: 11 feet (3.4 m) across, with 22-inch (56 cm) pupils

Nose: 20 feet (6 m) long

Mouth: 18 feet (5.5 m) wide

Cost to build: $990,000

Funded by: The U.S. government and private donors

Nickname: The Shrine of Democracy

Visitors per year: ~ 2 million

aquamarine — a transparent blue, blue-green, or green mineral that is used as a gem

East — the part of the world that includes the countries of Asia

Great Depression — a time from 1929 to 1939 when there was widespread unemployment in the U.S. and a major drop-off in the production and sale of goods

ideals — ideas that reflect standards or principles that people hope to achieve; excellent or perfect examples

igneous — a type of rock made when volcanic lava cools and solidifies

limestone — a kind of rock made up partly of the hardened remains of dead organisms; it is used widely in construction and cement-making

Louisiana Purchase — an 800,000-square-mile (2.1 million sq km) territory extending from the Mississippi River to the Rocky Mountains; America bought it from France in 1803

Panama Canal — a man-made waterway created from 1904 to 1914 through the Central American country of Panama to connect the Pacific and Atlantic Oceans

plumb line — a cord weighted on the end to hang down; it is used to determine depth or ensure that an object is vertical

protractor — an instrument used to measure angles; it is shaped like a semicircle and marked with the degrees of a circle

territories — areas of the U.S. that are not part of one of the 50 states and have their own lawmaking body; examples include Puerto Rico and Guam

West — the part of the world that includes the countries of Europe and North America

winches — machines used to raise or lower something with a rope or chain that is wound around a cylinder turned by a crank

INDEX